TRANSITION TO PHILOSOPHY VOLUME THREE

JOHANNES BERGFORS

chipmunkapublishing
the mental health publisher

All rights reserved, no part of this publication may be reproduced by any means, electronic, mechanical photocopying, documentary, film or in any other format without prior written permission of the publisher.

>Published by
>Chipmunkapublishing
>United Kingdom

http://www.chipmunkapublishing.com

Copyright © 2025 JOHANNES BERGFORS

TRANSITION TO PHILOSOPHY VOLUME THREE

THE WING-BIT

It's not even mine own, but whose it is I do not absolutely know, that piece of literature I happened to find in the mind's ear or hear floating round in the new air in my bedroom:

He found himself on a plane.

He found himself on a.

He found himself on.

He found himself.

He found.

P.

At the time I deemed it the property of Dr. Calculator Ptom, with whom I became bloodbrothers long ago. It is of course a concrete poem – hairless, featherless and ecstatic, perfectly formed in Visual if not Oral ways. Dr. Calculator Ptom (if that's whose it is) read philosophy at Cambridge, so that could be the sense of the P. There are nevertheless other "options." P, as Wittgenstein contends, could be "Proposition." Wittgenstein might say:

$P = \sim \sim P$

But what the proposition is, if that is the sense of the P, we do not know. I can see how the shape of the P completes the word-picture; but I can also see how a tragedy has happened, or a mistake been made. I believe poems like that are called "calligrammes."

It has been said that in my poetry-writing career, the wing-bit above is the only good bit in the whole of it. It's not the only report I have heard, for I have also heard that 'That Black Natural E' is a good poem, for instance, but it is a valid opinion. By now I have changed from "poet" to "philosopher" and can report that there is fairness that is airborne in the cloud.

But first let me tell you about my friend Dr. Calculator Ptom. My friend Dr. Calculator Ptom named one of my old bands, the band I was in at the time, Oedipus Wrecks upon hearing my songs. He used to say gnomic things like "the universe is a projection of the mind." "The G note is green on the guitar fretboard." "The song 'Born Slippy' is evidence dance can have a soul." "Poetry is untranslatable because of the music." "I was doing some thinking and realised Death is God." "Early Oasis is good for bittersweet, comedown energy." We boarded a train not knowing where it was headed in the middle of the Night in London. By now he is Dr. Calculator Thomas and the song is 'Born Slippery.'

So you could see the sense of P as the silent P that is the prefix to Ptom, as in "pterodactyl," that he knocked off in the end. He always said pretension was a good thing in art and called himself Ptom with a P; and maybe in growing up a bit he wished to get rid of the P and sent the wing-bit my way...

He found himself on a plane.

He found himself on a.

He found himself on.

He found himself.

He found.

P.

It was aloft in the sentient air. It came through me. I was the fingers. I was instructed by someone not physically in the room in writing the first line, then the second, then I followed suit, then at the end the interlocutor posited the P. But where was he going? Was he going on holiday? Already I start to see a piece of writing could emerge where the wing-bit is a bit like the Monolith from *2001: A Space Odyssey*, or else just a refrain.

He found himself on a plane.

He found himself on a.

He found himself on.

He found himself.

He found.

P.

What I find remarkable about it is the absence of bad writing. Martin Amis said good writing is only the absence of bad writing. The wing-bit may be the only exemplum on my laptop of writing that contains no bad writing.

When Dr. Ptom and I boarded the train not knowing where it was headed we ended up sleeping in a wood! We've had some adventures... I remember well the Latin trip where he got me into Tricky and I got him into the Smashing Pumpkins. He now thinks Billy Corgan one of the best lyricists as I think Tricky is too. If Tricky organised his lyrics as a book, with the lyrics in alphabetical order according to their names, I would say it would be true literature. Art tends to the Low not High End these days so I would hesitate to call it "High Art" but it would be good. We also went on holiday to Devon with all the songwriters of the year. We've been to Glastonbury too... all sorts of adventures.

Back in the day, Dr. Ptom always said people should sleep naked. That moment in the dark, naked, at the end of the day, reflecting, getting to sleep and dreams could be a philosophical moment – just you and the universe. Time to ask questions. Maybe time to turn to God. Time to project your mind into the future and into the past and still huddle round the present tense. In sleep our bodies are united again with beautiful, heartbroken, sentient, rosethirsty earth.

There was a school reunion once where I dyed my hair and turned up out of the blue with a guitar. Ptom then turned up and said "John! I had a dream last night you had dyed your hair and would turn up with a guitar!" The walls are thin. This is how Dr. Ptom g-a-v-e- me the present. The sense of P could be "present." It could also be possibility as in "a man of possibility." I could be one of those, or Ptom. I could go on for hours but I already hear someone say they preferred it when I used the wing-bit in a piece of appropriative writing called 'Moonpig.'

JOHANNES BERGFORS

MOONPIG

(an experiment in appropriative writing)

Moonpig got born. Are you in or out of the house? He proved you could incrementally affect the colour of white skin slightly through boyhood maths, be maths lies or the language of Nature.

He found himself on a plane.

He found himself on a.

He found himself on.

He found himself.

He found.

P.

Fleeing the world on a midnight plane, he found another planet. There was so much dust; he kicked up dust wherever his feet would fall and kept wondering "shouldn't I write that down?"

There was the breakfast of every snooker ball colour in James's bedroom for example. A plane exists on 2 dimensions including Time; a pyramid exists on 4 dimensions including Time; but to turn a plane into a pyramid is a one dimensional step – and did I mention I wanted to die?

The dust was endless.

Then there was the living spreadsheet – here have that! He knew it would've made the News: a flat, plastic rectangle with a pattern of evil, black eggs splurged on top appearing inside a jacket. He seems to remember throwing it away.

But by that stage Moonpig had already written a little book. In it he had stored the idea of "the ire ii net" in writing in the attic in 1989, which involved encrypting a scientific node to do with Gravity. In it he had also done what by now was thought of as the mad, addled maths for the new colour itself, also separated the pollen from its name in writing.

The maths in question is not that difficult to understand. To start with the embedded node in the boyhood book was that if the Gravity between earth and moon is instant and therefore enough to break light speed, a clock is still only as fast as a cheetah. That was why they got him to start encrypting it in a book called

2

MOONPIG

ENGLISH

E

and to continue encrypting it in a book called

ENGLISH

MOONPIG

HARECROFT HALL

1

At some point a + sign was put in for an F of scarf in the line:

"I have a scar+ that is red and black."

Then he wrote about how "I woke up at 1. o. clock," contrasting the number 1 and the first person pronoun. The splitting of the two books was the entry on number 2. For the number three he wrote

Colour circles red. How many circles?

Colour triangles blue. How many squares?

Colour oblongs orange. How many triangles?

Don't forget "when I was 4 I was on holiday in Sweden," he said, "and crashed my new bike into the nettles." Don't forget "my brother is five years old," and so on and so on. There was something for six in there and he went beyond it too.

Then it came in a dream, humbled him, the creature that waited out the war, and the other, upon the selling of his father's art dealing business at the fall of the Berlin Wall.

In the wake of becoming the witness, he had written a paper on the dinosaurs, ending with the line "last Autumn, two biologists announced they had cloned the DNA of a forty-million-year-old, extinct, stingless bee found in amber." That may be where we get the expression "the bee-line" from today.

He had also learned to play football. His first album was called *The Road To Heaven by Noj And The Mob*, containing inflections of Popperian epistemology, Miltonian theology and Backward Liquid Maths. He had grown very strange too: there was a line or mark or stripe or seam or tear up the front of what the Irish might call his forearm, which he discovered in the bath – and it didn't turn out to be the new colour in the end. He had still read the lesson from John in Eton College Chapel and did it better than the headmaster. He won the English and French Prizes. Now where else?

He learned smoking and drinking and night-walking at boarding school. He started to play guitar, his neophyte punk mnemonic for the strings of the electric guitar Even A Dick Gets Big Erections. Really?

It should also be known that before he had done his GCSE's he attained the face of stars with two friends in Eskdale. The phrase "to Boot" comes from that time he took his two friends, to Boot, Eskdale, where they attained the face of stars. The word "amazeballs" originated in his brain, around this time, 1998.

By then he was in a second band, Oedipus Wrecks, who gigged in London a few times. They had a song with the line "oceans smile with liquid eyes and fill themselves with rain." Already in 1998 they considered themselves to be Grime.

Moving schools again, he met Paul, fell in love with Flora, started a d.i.y. poetry magazine which was what they would call in Modernism "a mushroom mag" meaning transient and pop-up, meant to bypass the publication industry for imposing a stifling uniformity of styles and compromising poetry's purist, radical causes.

Her breath a poisonous magic.

He had also had a band called Secret Chord H who made it to the radio with a song called 'Dream With Open Eyes.' Secret Chord H was meant to be a metaphor for some experiential pleasure that lies unknown and beyond.

A Millennial school-leaver, Moonpig had also spoken against September 11th in 2000, predicted the hunt for the God Particle from looking at dust in a late ray angling in, foreseen what he now knows is to be called the white eyebrow, set aside an ideal for a book to write that two years later would be published by his University tutor in name and concept alike, but not before Moonpig wrote the highest-marked English Literature A-level exam essay in the nation.

Well, there were also musical concepts he was involved with in his youth. He started recording an album on binaural earphones, gained an effervescent mobile phone reverberating the rhythm of 'William Tell' through every technological inlet in the room before it rang... he had also had a project on healing a tape of its pause where cut and re-sealed in the reel; and they were tattooing his name on *Piper At The Gates of Dawn* because he was the witness.

That fourth band he was in, recording on earphones in Cambridge, were called The Flood, after a quote from Rimbaud. The quote is that "after the idea of the flood had subsided, the rabbit, in among the flowers, said a prayer to the rainbow through the spider's web." It is the first line of *Les Illuminations*.

Around this time, Moonpig had some very strange beliefs, or tenets in a belief-system:

- I. T. might stand for Instant Travel too

- Portability is the apotheosis of form

- It's impossible to write an anti-poem

- Lucy in the soul with demons might happen to be an actual substance

- Monopoly money should work on wine

- Poetry is the bike riding itself

and he expressed a desire to "plug my senses in the mains," as he sang vociferously on the binaural earphone recordings in The Flood.

At some point he decided he was going to be a teacher. He left The Flood and went to the foot of the Lakeland's oldest fell and embarked on a prodigious, counter-Rimbaudian program of meditation, dreamwork, detox, reading and exercise, inspired everyone to give up smoking, and coined the word co-imagination.

Well, when Moonpig went off to University as a mature student he went crazy. We're talking objects vanishing on the periphery of madness, books changing name, olfactory hallucinations, a plethora of voices, a montage of fifty bearded Muslim faces in the mirror, even an holographic horsecock wheeled into the bedroom… he still pressed on to get a degree.

At some point, the white eyebrow, telluric, preternatural and sublime, plugged into place in his back garden. It had been then that he remembered, a graduate now, the two weird specimens of boyhood, recognised he was the witness from some old book, and was formally diagnosed schizoaffective disorder, which will undoubtedly make it harder for him to be believed.

Large-scale skywriting at The Secret Garden Party did not go unnoticed. The pint glass exploding from thin air in the capital was but a piece of pollen in the pollen count. He got on an Eastend bus and flashed up a card with no money whereupon the reader said BACKPASS ATTEMPTED instead of NO MONEY.

Back in the north again, his dad whipped out a flower-press ending on cannabis and within a week Moonpig saw Flora from boarding school trotting on a horse in his own village, smirking, which was when he even became the poet to have formulated and articulated an idea...

A female's little fingernail clipping was poked between his bottom front teeth, he knew an inscape of blissful wings, built The Tower of magic books like one with smell and one a vanished line, cooked said cassette tape in the dark blue AGA, top oven, hottest one, worked for many years at a numinous, purple-bleeding PC screen, at some point falsified the Nirvana barcode || | |||| | || | ||||, upon the loss of his father, and also went and *made the discovery of a sheet where pictures grew...*

it had seemed to him to be portentous of the end of the chip. The pictures seemed to depict the lyric to one of his old songs too; but with the sheet belonging to his younger brother, he could not dictate that. So he knew for the first time what it was to lose.

Privation being the mother of imagery, loss being a portal of discovery, it was then that he attained visual radio, broadcasting dreams, swirling about his educated head. So he turned out to be a mystic in a way, or rather a seer.

If dog = pi times MC squared

it is because you wish to think him round;

and O is the key of the babbling unicorn

and its soul-assuaging sound.

Before he l-a-n-d-e-d on this Godforsaken, dust-ridden planet, Moonpig had also been in a fifth band: Black Hole Myths. It should also be documented that he had by then read *Ulysses* too, sought out healing in the form of Reiki for some event that happened years ago and was living in the house at the foot of the Lakeland's oldest fell Black Combe. The house had been rather cold. It had been Lockdown that had him fixed to that spot; then the war in Ukraine came along, leaking in the brain from afar, and it was like life had started to copy cheap action movies.

Now he was walking through endless dust… dull was this new planet. He feigned High Indifference to the new world, like standing alone in Nothingness to dictate the parameters of his own existence. Lighting bolts started to dagger down like part of a God Simulation.

He had to find a way back; so he built a machine, and called it Beth -

lest we fade before we have bloomed.

TRANSITION TO PHILOSOPHY VOLUME THREE

PHILOSOPHY OF DESPAIR

I don't think the correct sense of P is the Philosophy of Despair. It is nearer Pi's infinite decimal places. But as for the former I lie in bed. I am thinking of Radiohead on a rainy day. It is not raining but the day I am remembering was a rainy day. I have a feeling. It is late at night. Soon my mind is off and away on an adventure, or else a trained rat going round a circuit. I think how fragile life is; how unlikely the universe; how weird it is that everything is happening. It doesn't augur well that we are born the way we are, (for birth is traumatic for all concerned), and at the end lie underground with your pa; and in the meantime, all you hope to achieve is futile; our hopes and dreams comes to nothing. They all end up dust in the end. All our poetry is useless for we are all going to die. In fact space is likely to be emptied of the human form. So it all turns to dust. It is all meaningless.

This I would say is the philosophy of despair. If by some fluke you still believe in God despite it you might plead to him to present Nothingness instead of the universe next time. "Why is there something rather than nothing?" you ask yourself, in the philosophy of despair.

But Dr. Calculator Ptom wouldn't stand for it. He would remain an optimist, everlastingly upbeat. He would retain "good energy." Technically he was a Liberalist; and I would say Liberalism is the opening of all perceptions, all possibilities, and it leads to Hamlet's *harmatia* irresolution, whereupon pragmatism becomes the reactivation of an attitudinisation in that situation. Yes technically Ptom was a Liberalist but he was also an optimist. There was nothing craven, nihilistic or unseemly to the man. What a pleasure it was to spend time with someone so intelligent.

And in the end – w/r/t/ the philosophy of despair – if you can do something about it don't worry because you will; and if you can't do something about it, don't worry because there's nothing you can do about it. Hence a new dawn is lifted from the sea. Love is returned to white light/ white heat and re-forged and faith is restored. Dr. Ptom always liked the mishearing he heard in a song by Suede more than the lyric itself:

"We are the glitter on the trees,

not the litter in the breeze."

He also liked that Massive Attack song that he said "just sounded like a sunrise." What an aesthetic efficacy for a song: to make it sound like the dawn! He was right; when I hear that song now I think of the rising sun. So in Dr. Ptom we have a beacon of hope.

THE SONG

Now the guys want me to rewrite the one about the time we smoked a joint, Dr. Calculator Ptom and I, before the rugby match.

I was playing full-back.

The ball went up high in the air and I was underneath it.

I was underneath it and dropped the ball.

It wasn't like me at all.

I dropped it because I was still so befuddled from the joint.

The dads on the touchline were tutting, asking who was this inept player.

It was me; and my dad was also there.

He was embarrassed by me that day

because he was captain of rugby at his own school

and in every way the star player of the team.

So the lesson is not to get high before the Game.

Suddenly I remember that God is a game, that the game is based on permutation, that even a game of cards can be a rehearsal for death. That *The Lords And The New You Know Who* is also a game, a wide, yellow circle with death the pinpoint centre and the circumference closing in. Yet this is not a media-compression experiment dreamed up on LSD under a hot, Californian sun. This is not to say "he who controls the media controls evolution." This is not about chance collocations churning up evidence through the operation of a game.

I seem to remember we lost the match.

I seem to remember I was dropped from the team.

TRANSITION TO PHILOSOPHY VOLUME THREE

"CODSWALLOP"

There was one time I wrote Dr. Ptom a piece about philosophy and animals. It was after my degree when I went back down to live in London, was on the street for a bit, and got into an emergency hostel. I started with a Preface delimiting that it had been transcribed from defaced bank notes which was nice – then kicked in with the imperative

"Take out your Lords and see in all directions at once."

He's probably still got it (alas.) It went on about how certain naturalistic observations could've had cinema as the Transforming Agent, and I was stoned when I wrote it, and it wasn't very good, so that may be why Dr. Ptom "sent" the wing-bit, if he did, to silence the feast.

He found himself on a plane.

He found himself on a.

He found himself on.

He found himself.

He found.

P.

"Pleasure" is the word that comes to mind. WH Auden never lost track of the idea that a poem should induce pleasure. I may have forgotten it down the years; and pleasure may be what was lacking in the piece I sent Ptom. But where would he be flying to at this time of Night? That is, are we to launch into an investigation, and a fiction at once?

Dr. Ptom's names in his novel are like Pynchon: over-determined. He's one of the only people that I have met that had even higher literacy than me at school. And when we got to the wood and slept there what did we dream of? Under a pile of fallen leaves? And what if the wing-bit wasn't him? I mean I hear a lot of voices, prompts, triggers, cues, minion, staff, quavers, "onjects," syllabubbles, sonic machinations at the periphery of sound and people too. Some of them know how to have their way with my writing as if my laptop were the centre of the world. You start to hair as opposed to hear. You could call them "Squalia" as opposed to Qualia!

NOTE ON HOW MY YOUTH HAS FLOWN

I remember when I was living in London for GCSE's and attending the boys' school Habs, I would wake in my great bunk bed with a feeling of butterflies in my stomach, a feeling of tremendous excitement and hope on a Saturday morning.

Today I woke up, aged 43, somehow still alive, and checked my e-mail and found the publishers had accepted amendments to *Transition To Philosophy* as a book and the publication of *Transition To Philosophy Volume Two*.

When I was doing my English Literature and Creative Writing degree at Lancaster it was said that reading English is a "pointless activity," and I imagine reading philosophy the same in terms of the marketplace but not the inner richness of soul and life and experience you get from it.

I think back to when I first attended Lancaster and saw a poster advertising philosophy books for sale… some bright spark had written on the poster "yes but are they real?"

"Real" was a property privileged by John Keats.

I think the philosophers at Lancaster started off doing about "Impartials" – truths not given to self-interest or bias.

Anyhow I never wake with that feeling of butterflies in my stomach anymore, now that I live in the countryside full time, now that my youth has flown.

And what exactly is this property "real?"

We were always taught in Modernism that reality has become untenable.

Even science has come round to thinking there is no such thing as Objective reality.

But this is not about butterflies in the stomach anymore.

A parcel from Amazon arrives for James – what is it?

I check Facebook for news of my mother's holiday in Finland.

I check my G-mail for news of the book I am publishing.

I read further news on the BBC news website.

These things wouldn't have been possible twenty or so years ago.

There are people alive that are already adults that weren't even born when the Towers came down!

One minute, all the footballers are older than you, the next minute you are older than them all.

Then your favourite band – Radiohead – retire – a band who have been with you through your youth – whose singles you remember coming out in days where you went to Festivals like Glastonbury, Essential, T-in-the-Park.

And you've lost contact with your old friends.

And you don't have an audience for your poetry anymore, so the poetry shrivels.

And you can't quite look back at any concrete achievement.

I await the publication of *Transition To Philosophy*!

And maybe the transition is not complete until the book of that name comes out right?

Another cup of tea goes down.

This is the Land of Swaying Abeyance where the long grass blows in the sea-salt breeze.

You never see me drinking in a cocktail bar up here.

I'm either in bed reading or at the kitchen table writing on my laptop.

This is also the Land of Propitious Mud but I rarely if ever get out there walking anymore.

I used to walk A LOT and for large periods was fit; now I walk never at all and am FAT.

My hair is long like a hippy and tied in a ponytail round the back.

I think back to the days of my youth as poet and songwriter…

AS A SHORT STORY

He looked about him. He realised nobody onboard the plane could understand how the plane worked, how it was up in the air. There was a guy sitting next to him that could've been a bouncer, a spy, an agent. It was a plane coming back from Italy to Manchester via Germany, so it was a German plane. It turned out though that the joke is sky-high: the German plane was taken over by the Irish, hijacked that is, just so they could land it safely! For those of a mentally ill disposition this is a hectic thing; but my dad would've loved it. Eventually the plane landed safely in Manchester. He – who I would like to call James – had made it back from his brother Robert's wedding to England.

He went and found the car and drove back to Cumbria. The news was on the radio. The world contained several wars – Russia had attacked the Ukraine. There was also war in the Gaza Strip. An awakened social conscience cared but recognised it was not his problem, not even his own language, so there was nothing he could do. If only there was some kind of... if only they could use his big brother John, who had attained the face of stars which was scripted in the Bible, to design a plan for a shock-proof world. Part of that would surely involve an experiment into the international language alphabet. But if there was still war in the world John's ideal of bringing back the Summer of Love had failed. John – James's older brother – had made a brilliant speech, or several, in the den in the barn in 2000, outlining his philosophy – ideals, ambitions, inventions, aphorisms, prophecies. He was tuned in. He had spoken against September 11th for example, using his own brain, in 2000.

When James got home, he made a cup of decaff tea and thought about continuing his novel, a sci-fi novel about a spaceship. It was already 20 files, each with 30,000 words on. Let's hope the Feds don't take objection. He sat and tried to think of what to write, dying to get a good book done. Bright ideas were forthcoming too. Gone were the years when he was trying to become a philosopher. Now it was older brother trying to be a philosopher and he himself, being left-handed and more creative, was working with sci-fi. He was already the author of the new da Vinci circle, that may have left a mark in terms of the sheet where pictures grew, but wanted more. He may have deemed the sheet an act of vandalism. If we printed John's lyrics that were depicted in the sheet, that was not to head in the direction of philosophy. What we could show is a couple of University poems from John that might contain the seed-consciousness of the sheet, even if only unconsciously.

THAT BLACK NATURAL E

[spoken word narrative for B minor]

Where once I wandered far and wide

on a field-file, a file-field,

a fenceless farm without

security alarm where all hearts bleed

and all arts breed, now Hell

is very quiet, unadvertised.

McBreastmilk,

McBreastmilk,

don't feed your kids.

Gentle face erasing cream,

smear it in and let it sink

down through the pores of your skin

to erase your deepest down dirt.

O stars the government

that truly speaks for us!

Get an extra kid for free

when you spend 99p.

Freefall 0800 down

your own black hole pupils.

Maybelline you maybe only make-believe

you may be the true mating queen of the hive,

may mad vampires stalk you,

stalking walls walk through

your vagrant dreams.

I see state of head

is more than Head of State.

Monster Munch can

always gobble up your food.

Cancerel can always

sweeten the stewed-

carfume coffee we sip in

this liminal afterlounge.

It's getting cramped

as a tin of beans in here.

In emergency please

break glass and exit.

Credits at the end of innocence

are falling like numberless lists

of fallen autumn leaves.

Snatched handfuls of light

come to nothing in the dark room.

There must be a use for

this dust amounting.

There's nothing like digging

a meaningless hole as if to cure the

spiralling lethargy of Hell...

and when I went into the

woods to bury my soul,

all the trees knelt down.

O perpetual orgasm of the sun!

Privation is the mother of imagery.

Prayers, ghosts and

e-mails chatter on

the ego-loss breeze.

The chitchat in the solipsistic

kitchen of fiction is 'phatic'.

My new, motley fridge magnet

letters contain no question

mark in the pack but the first

qualification of Modernism

is enquiry and furthermore

wilful ignorance is a sin.

Meanwhile outside the

fallen Autumn leaves

are where bears have

dipped their feet in pots of paint

and danced across the threshold

of the paving stones.

Water clears its throat from the tap.

Gunpowder was only invented

for fireworks and a firework

is a champion sperm nosing up

blind to explode bright and wonderful

deep-sea creatures in the Ancient Night.

The world is a cool, bejewell'd

marble snug in Holy Orbit

suckling on a mother sun.

Supposedly there is soon

to be New Atlantis on the moon.

The cure for cancer

sustains your heart.

Robbed by a bastard vending machine,

somewhere a tramp drinks paint-stripper

to cleanse the doors of perception,

a drunkard attacks a wall

on an otherwise empty street,

a policeman forces himself

to come with a gun.

Hey salesman

slow down

with that

fast-food.

I don't mind

waiting here

for a year.

(2002)

JOHANNES BERGFORS

SKUNKFOOT

(spoken word narrative to go over a drone of E)

Portability still seems the Apotheosis of Form: sometimes I can be walking along on a sunny day when I jump from the jungle to the Arctic to the Sahara. Mutation in consciousness itself, truth too simple to understand, these are gesture-without-motion-bones, like sadness gene and dreaming gland. It's not impossible to write an anti-poem. Love is not a mechanistic set of rules. Love was once aligned with madness, fever and intoxication. Love became grouped with language not God. Love became a tough word-combination. Love has no ego as everyone knows, and so it goes and so it grows. I for one think Lucy in the soul with demons may happen to be an actual substance. Travelling south, as I read Rimbaud, a rainbow smashed a railway train window. A baby cannot trip without memories... I remember "every atom ate our eyes." Our eyes: they are ingrown in the ocean's bellyful of wine, down in the seabed-orchard. There is angelic music inborn in the inner ear; but those whom the Gods wish to drive mad are sent the end of 'Bike' in their heads and madness is not something to be Romanticised as a return to Purity. Impunity seems more what the poet wants. He likes to float on the artifice of organic emotions through synthetic sounds, and is into exploring alternative histories suppressed by the overarching meta-narrative. For plastic surgery of the soul there are libraries. Poetry is the bike riding itself. Monopoly money will get us well, Monopoly money will get us bread, she picks the blue tac off the wall and says "my T-shirt is red". I put my wounds up on bright flags; I take the angel up the arse. To plug my senses in the mains might engage [!00 %] of my brains. It's all about a permanent reactivation of the Glastonbury Festival spirit. John Tucker is taking acid again. Money shags in the dark. Thoughts of one's greatness only diminish one's greatness. Skunkfoot is putrid demons excreted through stone. Love an army of fire. Fire needs some incentive to rise up. Shall I touch my heart with a red Bic biro? When all the air in outer space is consumed… The bed in the wood, it was definitely a whore's, with solar spike I can use the Force, with R2D2 I cleanse my doors, I'm just trying to win my Star Wars. I'm starting to think in five musical parts at once. The Anon Throwaway as a new form could become an alternative currency to rival with money for the role of the real. Formal education is not for everyone. The yellow DogMuckels M atop the pole in the industrial park is the postmodern churchspire in the spiritual vacuum. Postmodernism is theme dissolved into message. Giant killers are frozen peas in the microwave. I look into the mirror though I shouldn't pool my sources. I'm not going to die at the age of twenty seven, watch the dreamtapes on repeat from a golden seat in Heaven. The heart beats to the rhythm of one. A fiver is surely cheese and onion flavour. Cataclysm is catalyst for the old cat that sat on the map of sound, just because the world is very round. If there were paper under my heart there would be writing on it and it would be art. I might ding it in compressed Space Age seconds.

(2002 - 2003)

JOHANNES BERGFORS

FUSION

So we see that even as I close down on the condition of philosophy I try and scintillate the reader. It's almost like writing a fusion. Professor John Schad of Lancaster University said fusions are the future: since English and Creative Writing Departments merged, students in either discipline can be released with the beautiful mandate of writing an essay as if getting gradually more drunk. Fusions are also the past – if for example the musical scales were codified by scientists. So you can expect people to write philosophy in poetry – to write in ways of cross-pollination between genres.

Anyhow, by now I am sitting with it all in my idyll. I am back with a bang from a strange planet, a detour into outerspace, clenching the moment now while it lasts. There may only be one poem I ever wrote that was any good that I have not showed you yet herein or in the transition to philosophy series – for by now it is a series. By now they may come like Proust, one after the other, in a box-set in a future bookshop. That's what I hope.

Yes I am back from a strange adventure. I didn't notice the thunder last night even though it was loud, because I was asleep. I heard about the thunder this morning from another who witnessed it in wakefulness. And back with a bang, I can report that Adventures are good. Neil Curry says a poem is the opposite of a bus ticket – it takes you on an inward journey. Dr. Ptom and I had many adventures. We used to smoke pot together in London in our teens. Literature could be said to be a vehicle. I heard it that religion is a vehicle too, but literature is a mode of transport for the imagination. That's why I like Dr. Ptom's wing-bit. He even sent it without any fingers. I just did the fingers in the wing-bit. Skilful, dextrous fingers I have; and a finely attuned ear; and a noble heart; and a beautiful mind. It was voices that told me to "do the P" for my new *Transition To Philosophy Volume Three* - but they may have just meant "do the Future State."

I can't tell if I ever wanted to give Dr. Calculator Ptom head or not – because I love women at the same time. My sister Hannah and her bf, meanwhile, said to me I cannot be the witness from T*he Lords And The New Creatures* AND a government scientist who helped invent the net at seven at the same time. I was though, and so efforts have been made to simultaneously renounce my position as witness AND eschew the governmental side of things. My brother James says not to renew my boyhood maths and science. We already have a book called *The Sunset Child* by John Tucker.

Now I am going to show you an excerpt of writing from a time of substance abuse, while living in Millom. I thought I was hosting the Mind Hearing Voices Group from my own flat, alone in the room. It just goes to show the levels of extrasensory perception getting very high in the Digital Age.

JOHANNES BERGFORS

FEMINISATION OF P

"I deem the wing-bit," someone says "to be about cutting out cancer." It certainly has an air of surgical precision in its neatness! It seems to say "leave me free." And what would happen if it were feminised?

She found herself on a plane.

She found herself on a.

She found herself on.

She found herself.

She found.

P.

It might even be said to be about female masturbation that way. I never examined sexuality in the wing-bit previously, but there is probably a pornographic reading. There is also the Popperian sense of P1 to TT to EE to P2, which is an epistemological process, that I feel obliged to mention, as if I were writing a textbook, I who know so little about the chosen metier of philosophy, I who was Rebel Without A Pause when Dr. Ptom was busy reading.

I'm glad we feminised it. And where is she going? Is she going on holiday? Is she going to Portugal? She would look over the patchwork quilt below very briefly, and those pointing up, if they noticed a vapour trail, would remark at the insignificance. Then the plane might cross the sea! But where she is going we do not know. This could be an opportunity to bring up something I have mentioned before as an aesthetic anti-system.

It could be a Philosophy Theme Park. Or a Philosophy computer game. When my dad was dying he whipped out a flower-press ending on cannabis given to him by my mum. Around the time I saw a beautiful lass from boarding school, called Flora, trotting on a horse in the village, smirking. I decided if a flower-press ending on cannabis = a dialysis a love poem hoping to impress poor Flora = a motor. I probably wasn't the first to formulate and articulate such a pretext, as Flora herself has probably been living with it all her life, and other poets have cottoned on too, to this quasi-Rimbaudian anti-system. It occupied me for a long time and keeps cropping up even as I try to make the transition to philosophy count. On the table is an empty crisp packet – that too would be part of the dialysis (which extends beyond the end of the world and the emptying of space of the human form.)

DOWNLOADING THE LOWDOWN OF DOWNTIME

So. Here I am (   ). Our house. The solipsistic kitchen of fiction. Writing. I have just had a kebab and a half – James and I got three to share – from Caspian's Take-away in Millom. I have also been talking to my mother who made some Frankfurters for herself. She says the best food in Millom is from Mmmmm... Hungry. She is right – their pizzas and burgers for example. But that is what we had yesterday. Writing of yesterday's food may be the Dorian Mode of the witness I once was but today is another day. Mum says so far this Transition to Philosophy has been Cartesian. If you still want me to renew what I have done for you, it will become a document all about madness. There are still people trying to clinch the last little bit, and own it, even though it is mine. Time does not pass but evaporate. Things live inside onions of themselves. Galloping water would be a cool thing to say. Please God, please look after all my friends and family, let them all have happy lives, lives full of love and happiness, and devoid of fear and pain and violence, violence both emotional and physical, for violence is wrong. May there never be violence here again. Amen.

PLENTY

Plenty, which comes from Latinate etymology meaning "full," could be my final answer as to the sense of the P. Over the last few months I have written *Transition To Philosophy*, also *Transition To Philosophy Volume Two*, and now seem to be writing *Transition To Philosophy Volume Three*. If all goes according to plan, they will each be published, and I will have done enough. This is just to say that what is contained herein is sufficient; and it should not be "put in the bin" be it by the Feds or the fire-dance because that would be evil. It is Fascist dictatorships that do that to books. When a Fascist dictatorship comes into power the first thing they do is close libraries and burn books because books are access to knowledge. If the Feds don't know this I would find that surprising because one would hope they are not actual Fascists and so if I were to place a bet, I would say that the books will survive, because I give the benefit of the doubt to the potential destroyer of my literature. So we see I needed to start again as Johannes Bergfors where before was John F B Tucker; and inherent in using the pen-name is an overthrowing of the predominant brain hemisphere and conscious self-censor. I get to look back on and poke fun at the scurrying around as a poet and song writer – as but an act of folly – and enjoy middle age from this vantage point of being a philosopher now. It's not just about identity but seeing and thinking clearly.

JOHANNES BERGFORS

P FOR PLOT-STRESS

Well, we haven't been to the Oedipus Wrecks gig yet – the band that Dr. Calculator Ptom named upon hearing my juvenile songs. I won't convince you they are Blake but maybe Rimbaud. Before the gig Dr. Ptom got on stage with OEDIPUS WRECKS written on his chest and pulled up his top, to show the crowd that was where the band name originated. It was a brilliant precursor to a brilliant gig, whose set-list I can show you now...

But waaaaaaait! Let's go back to the wood where we ended up on the night we boarded a train not knowing where it was headed. Dr. Ptom and I sleeping under a pile of leaves. We found a portal on the leafy floor, and opened it. There was a light switch and some steps going down into the heart of the earth. We followed the steps for about five minutes and came to a door. We opened the door and were let in to a bright-lit room. It was the Nobel Prize Ceremony! There was someone in there giving their Nobel Prize winning lecture... it was boring and time to reflect on mine own. I don't have much of a contention myself. Even if I wrote the blueprints for the internet, others still did more. Even if I tried the maths for the new colour, you'd have to see the private mark it made. Dr. Ptom is very sobering when he suggests that after all I have been through – attaining the face of stars! – I've never done anything to deserve a Nobel Prize. It can seem counter-intuitive when you lead a life like mine. I can run you through my science if you like...

TRANSITION TO PHILOSOPHY VOLUME THREE

PRELUDE

I was thrown blind into the world of science. Science knows, but also loves. John also loves. John loves science and all his friends and family. Hey, I once wrote the word "entropy" backwards with a dot between each letter if that means anything to you. Personally I am yet to find a meaning for it but have traipsed all the way back to the first, unformulated spark of appetence in Nothingness preceding Creation to try and give it meaning. No such thing as far as I can tell. No, there is no "entropy backwards." Nothing for the term to name. That might even be Tucker's constant!

Should you need to see some numbers at this stage of the day already, I would only suggest the equation for hanging your coat on the primary school wall:

$$+ x \; \tfrac{1}{2} = -$$

Is there any more basic way of expressing not only that energy is lost in transfer but that positive and negative form a cohesive unity?

Anyhow, my latest epiphany is that the substance crinoline can be grown; or at least maybe, maybe crinoline can be synthesised in evolution. It is a revelation derived from reading my father's last notebook. I understood, or entertained, reading it, that crinoline was a part of the material of a kind of "living spreadsheet" I discovered in my early boyhood, around the time of the dawn of the world wide web. I was only 8 and it was already Observation number two.

They were days of acid-rain which you don't hear of so much anymore but which reminds me of a stance I have: I believe it specious that the effects of acid and of acid-rain on an imaginary species = the same, nothing, if there can be no more ultimate proof of something being real than saying it was imagined.

That's not to say the living spreadsheet was not real: it was a fully "reified" and tactile object which I did not keep on account of it looking grim; but thinking I know now after all these years what the material was, I thought it a duty to science, to Man, to bring the revelation to the written word.

My life has actually been full of events of scientific interest which warrant narrative. Not all of them are as disgusting as the living spreadsheet I assure you, which should've been left to soak in water, but wasn't. I do intend to take you on a crash course through the main moves I made to show you how I must've been crying out for the condition of science from a young age, to dignify things.

TRANSITION TO PHILOSOPHY VOLUME THREE

OUTLINE OF LIFE EVENTS THAT LEAD TO THE CONDITION OF SCIENCE

Although I have said it all before I will say it all again, and there is good reason to say it here and now and real and feeling – to talk about my life - even if it seems quite tiresome in terms of the narrative unto the reader. Well, as you by now know if you have read my CV: when I was only seven, and liked the film *All Dogs Go To Heaven*, I scribed a little book that performed at least four scientific functions: it encrypted a scientific notion concerning Gravity, storing the idea of the net in writing in the attic to give it a chance to grow around the world; calibrated an algorithm that sublimates numbers and letters on a cellular level to see if the new colour, I think, could be rendered as a cellular mark; and separated the object 'pollen' from its name - and I did not consciously know, even though it was writ with my own right hand.

Some might say that's already enough or too much. Then at eight I made two Naturalistic Observations I didn't understand… if one was the breakfast of every snooker ball colour in James Joyce's bedroom, the latter was the plastic spreadsheet. If I had to conjure an "abstract" out of being the one to make those Observations I would simply say in talking about *The Lords And The New You Know Who* by Jim Morrison coming true something "kinetic" becomes something "static." It's the same as John Barnes's sensational goal against Brazil. We cannot give the uncertainty back to the moment when we watch the Action Replay. We know the ball is going in. Something kinetic becomes something static.

Yes, by the age of eleven I was "incrementally" marked by the maths of the new colour on the hand even though it didn't turn out to be the new colour in the end. My siblings and I wrote *The Road To Heaven by Noj And The Mob*. We sang of the dog going round and round chasing own tail!

Leaving Prep School, I soon enough came into possession of a cassette cut and resealed in the flimsy reel and an ideal to do away with the pause. That was one experiment back then. It being Pearl Jam 'VS' I suppose the experiment was in organising a poetry machine in perpetual motion. At fifteen I formed a second band called Oedipus Wrecks. My mnemonic for the strings was indeed Even A Dick Gets Big Erections. I also led two friends to the face of stars. We were three gathered in the name that Night so it could be something from the Bible but there are other options including collective hallucination, including a vision scripted in *The Lords And The New You Know Who*. By now I had started reading it.

I formed Secret Chord H and an Anon love poetry magazine while still at school, sweet sixteen. Then at eighteen years old in the year 2000, and not unlike Democritus of the Ancient Greeks, I foresaw the hunt for the God Particle from looking at dust in a late ray of light angling in. I was a fully tuned-in prophet on other fronts too, even savant but have learned I cannot necessarily say what I want. I admit that I did entertain the idea that the witness from *The Lords And The New Creatures* by Jim Morrison *might have to become the missing link to the super-human corridor in evolution* – but it may not be my own thesis.

I envisioned our Plough alignment happening, but got the address well wrong, saying "maybe in India" as opposed to my back garden. I set aside an ideal for a book called *The Scientific Papers* about it all that would be classed as "a series of findings into itself, into the concept of art and science as a single discussion of perception."

Among the prophecies I spouted many ideas for inventions, many aphorisms, many artistic ambitions. That year I wrote the highest-marked English Literature A-level exam essay in the nation at 100%.

My fourth band The Flood recorded an album or even algorithm on binaural earphones… the earphones were my idea to invent, back in the den in the barn, which was never mentioned once during the band because it wasn't me that implemented it. Already some of these things seem scientific, these motifs, this Excellent News. When writing a portfolio for Warwick University, furthermore, I entertained that I. T. might stand for Instant Travel too, that Portability might be the apotheosis of form…

The Towers came down, appalling us all or at least my friend Paul. I did feel the psychosis in my brain burn and burn. Still, I had little recollection of the barn where I had foreseen and spoken against it to the day using my own brain; and was persuaded at length, against my own instincts, to continue playing in the binaural earphone band.

Attending Warwick University, in 2002, I found my teacher, Professor David Morley, whom it would seem was a reasonable man, had just brought out *The Scientific Papers* and with an almost-verbatim classification to mine own. When it happens in sheep it is called morphic resonance and when it happens in academia it is uncanny imbrocation.

My first mobile, it reverberated the rhythm of 'William Tell' through every technological inlet in the room before it rang. I wrote a paper about whether or not Lucy in the soul w/ demons even happens to be an actual substance. With no degree, I returned to the band in my Gap Year haunt of Cambridge and promised on the binaural album recorded on earphones I'd "plug my senses in the mains."

Leaving the band, I coined the neologism "co-imagination," before attending a second university, Lancaster, where I got a First despite mental illness. My dissertation was on the scientist-poet David Morley. I attested to our Holy Cow, the white eyebrow, the alignment of the Plough, the Plough honed in to align for a beautiful rhythm change in the White House around that time.

I attended the Secret Garden party after and found real skywriting; gravitated down south, attesting to a pint glass exploding from thin air in the capital. I found my name on *Piper At The Gates of Dawn*, as if some sensory overlay had grown as naturally as grass.

Returning north again, I built The Tower out of books I had gained that seemed to exhibit signs of natural magic, like one emanating the redolent smell of perfume, and another that seemed to have lost a line. I worked at a numinous, purple-bleeding PC screen in an experiment into post-humanism. I found the tape I mentioned to be a successful fusion and listening in to the suggestion of the wind cooked it in the dark blue AGA's top oven.

When my dad died, and the purple-bleeding screen in the same instant, I discovered the sheet where pictures brown and blue simply bloomed or maybe grew. It could be portentous of the end of the chip. That was also when my boyhood book emerged which only now do I start to understand in terms of long storage. Then it was time to falsify the Nirvana barcode, and nor did I forget to extirpate every trace of recognition from the mind, unloose the mind of form, method-act every adjective in 'Howl' to attain visual radio, broadcasting dreams.

Throughout that sequence of events I found it impossible to gain even 1p and my friends on both the right and the left deem it that that is not fair; but it is not my business to complain about money. It's part of the reason we are thinking of selling. Sometimes we deem it fair if I get to keep the air. Up here the air is very clear, I mean fresh, for it is the light that is clear; but down in the town of my birth the air is not so good.

It eventually became time to publish books; but for some strange, unknown reason my computer was broken on the night before I was due to publish my first collection: *Rose Petals In The Ashtray*. So I had to go downstairs in the night-time and use my mother's ancient PC; so the first collection became half-remembered scraps instead of what I had. I got the name *Rose Petals In The Ashtray* from my dying dad and didn't know its meaning; so it was about innocence – but it was terrible what came out. In the version that went out there, there was a line missing from the first poem in the name of revision that made a good poem bad; then the second poem came from before it in the initial writing order. In the end it irritated rather than pleased me to have it out there, so soon enough I had it un-published, so there isn't really a start to my much-anticipated career.

Some further books were brought out especially in self-publishing on Amazon but they were building on nothing, no starting point, and only saw me messing it up further.

Binaural Songbook

57 Paintings For Art Therapy

The Field of Rock N Roll Science

John Tucker's Schooldays: A Spreadsheet Poem

Another 57 Paintings for Art Therapy

The New Beat

The Effect of Global Warming On The Unicorn

Word For Stained Glass Windows

154 Shakespearean Sonnets

In time to come I started again with the publisher *Chipmunka* when some succubus swooped down and got me to arrange my songs in a book called *Soundcloud Rain*, dressing me up to look like

Beethoven, when really I am not that musical as evinced by actually listening to the recorded material which you can on Bandcamp and Soundcloud.

After *Soundcloud Rain* came my boyhood proof, *The Sunset Child*, which in reality, back in 1989, was also when I "wrote the elephant" at seven but even in publishing that I missed off a crucial component part that goes at the start and shows I really was "writing the elephant."

Teacher rite elephant nite

everything lite lesson love

learn tell everyone Esso orange.

Without it the whole dynamic functionality of the boyhood proof is quite meaningless – and I missed it off because the proof had been stolen in its original, handwritten form before I had finished typing it up. Nevermind, eh?

Then I got to bring out *Breath Trapped In Heaven*, which was strictly all love poems; and I felt it could've been miles better as a book but it did at least strive to stop the war. There was still proper no start to the career, no first collection to be a foundational level in an eventual Collected Works, which probably won't come out by now, which seems a waste of the face of stars, and all those other things I got up to.

Then came *Brave New Tense* which only loaned a word from my mother – who can write off the top of her head in a way that quietly, discretely Taps the beck in the back. In *Brave New Tense* there was a bit of that going on, as if to bypass a need for a tract on Universal Human Rights.

SCIENCE SAYS

Science STILL says to only keep my falsification of the Nirvana barcode and my brother's notion about <BEE>. The latter is not mine; and once again, the former refers to that occasion when I made the Nirvana barcode to be but the beat of 'Scentless Apprentice' by Nirvana tapped out in approximate barcode shape using the tool of the qwerty keyboard.

I actually did have a mobile phone that buzzed off before it rang, through every technological inlet in the room, telly, stereo, laptop, air. So I wrote that down – that monochromatic drone – somehow - and it became a song that falsified the Nirvana barcode through bastardisations and mishearings of other people's songs, that nevertheless worked as a piece of music unto itself, sustaining narrative, meaning and musicality all at once. It has been called as good as Rachmaninov and goes as follows...

Di di dit di di dit di di dit dit dit

Di di dit di di dit di di dit dit dit

Di di dit di di dit di di dit dit dit

Bring bring

bring bring

"Hello?"

Gold member, you're the one,

the one with the heart of gold

Vowels, pure vowels

Immanuel Kant

will come to thee

with immanence

You come home smacked up you come

d/ d/ d/ down

grooving up slowly

d/ d/ d/ down

grooving up slowly

d/ d/ d/ down

grooving up slowly

yeah yeah yeah

yeah yeah yeah

yeah yeah yeah

boom

boom

boom

boom

boom

how did we get down here from flat-top

wide tunnel cities self driving cars

bears in the moon and liquor and drugs

and whisky baaaaaaaaaaaars

boom shanka, you're the one,

the one with the sonic boom

knickers knickers faster than lightning

skin up fall out of bed

and did those feet

in ancient times

rain down, rain down,

come on raindown

and walk the sun

fatter, hippier, less well connected

always walk the hallways

down to create my own

and in the meantime

and in the meantime

I'll do the monkey bars with my legs

manic depression has enraptured my name

don't know what I want but I just want shame

don't know what I want but I just won't shave

rainy waif, rain always,

lay back and dream

on a rainy waif

now I know how Kurt Cobain sang

oh now I know how Kurt Cobain sang

no more laaaaaaaaaa la's

removal van canes will be turned into furniture

we're thinking of putting Tricky's name on the front sir

you never see me dead near an inch of closure

|| | |||| | || | |||| 909 and 693 are wings

"and a record made of sound

goes round and round, conveying

music to the speaker through the stylus,"

says the radio as I turn it on.

Well, although there is no

such thing as the Nirvana barcode

it opens up a discussion about

the Telepathic Walkie Talkie, how

if barcode is rain barcode is phone...

and at least I have

the grace to come

back and say that the

extinction of consciousness

has no monetary value.

It is past dawn

and I see that

that first mobile

phone has gone.

(2015)

A NOTE ON MY FIRST NUMBER

The encrypted node in the boyhood work, meanwhile, was that if the Gravity between earth and moon is instant and therefore enough to break Light-speed a clock is still only as fast as a cheetah.

I see now that it was probably, probably government scientists who, for the sake of long storage, when the idea of the net needed storing in writing, got me to begin encrypting that with a text called

2

JOHN TUCKER

ENGLISH

E

and to continue with a second text called

ENGLISH

JOHN TUCKER

HARECROFT

1

"but then again who knows."

The split was not even but asymmetrical like one was on and one was off. It was like spotting the flaw in Einstein. It was like saying if you write Einstein backwards it implies the breaking of light speed. It was even like saying even if we invent a time machine that can equal light speed we can only go back in time because the future hasn't happened yet.

At some point, after the Einsteinian bit, a + sign was put in for the F of 'scarf' in the line

"I have a scar+ that is red and black."

Then there was a discussion of the struggle between 'Good and Evil' in a piece where

"I woke up at 1 o. clock."

In other words the first person pronoun and the time 1 o'clock were being contrasted.

It is not clear if the splitting of the two books happened next, for the number 2 in the sequence, but I think so. In terms of the number three, there was also my maths book where in among the numbers you find a three line poem going

Colour circles red. How many circles?

Colour triangles blue. How many squares?

Colour oblongs orange. How many triangles?

To read it all you'd only need to go and get a copy of what by now I know helped invent the net but which at the time of publication I did not know helped invent the net. It's called *The Sunset Child.* People have said the best one in it is called 'My Dad.'

It ascends, counting up, through others numbers - 4 is a bike crash in Sweden, when I am but 4 years old. 5 is my brother Dr. Robert's age when I was writing. 6 is a psychedelic story about drinking some lemonade and shrinking until I am but 6 inches tall. In that piece I also look at my watch – and find "it was 6. 58 and 37 seconds so we all ran as fast as we could towards the sofa."

So there is a variety of ways to incorporate a number in the numerical ascent, including ages, times of day, inches, dates, and more.

It strikes me that I might as well run you through regional variations in Korean cuisine, or describe a river's journey through varying and variegated ages of rock. The way I left it, calibrating an algorithm that sublimates numbers and letters on a cellular level to see if the new colour could be attained in a cellular way, it was just about counting...

sometimes I wonder if I can check my own biology – in terms of how much I grew or did not grow – to assess whether the encrypted node in the boyhood book is true or not. You only need to go on

Youtube and find a video to find out that gravity, in having no motion, can not be said to break the speed of light, only warp and bend the fabric of spacetime. If it didn't grow I would say the encrypted notion was wrong; if the mark was not the new colour I would say the experiment into the maths of the new colour failed.

The truth is it did grow but not a great deal: I went from being very well hung by nature to not so big by nurture; and the mark didn't turn out the new colour in the end; and semen spills like silver water; and still, the internet works.

THE LIVING SPREADSHEET

At eight years old, then, I made the two Observations, one a breakfast of every snooker ball colour in James Joyce's bedroom, the other the living spreadsheet.

W/r/t the latter, I tried on a jacket under the stairs and got a sense something was wrong and took it off and looked inside… "mum!" I cried up the wooden stairs. "There's something disgusting growing in this jacket!"

It could be described as a flat, plastic rectangle with a un-naturally regimented pattern of black stuff splurged on top.

I left the room to see if it would still be there when I went back; and it was; and so I decided to put the whole jacket in the bin.

I heard later, years later, it was called "Grand-darth's Ship" and took its Taxonomic Genus from one of my own seven year old poems.

As stated I gather from dad's last notebook that the plastic material might have been crinoline. Crinoline might have been the missing ingredient – the key part of the jigsaw, my knowing of which has propitiated that I bring the discovery to the realm of readership.

How dad knew when he'd never seen it I don't know but I believe him – it makes sense – as if he got it from grand-dad.

The poem Grand-darth's Ship was about how my grand-dad Don became a deep-sea diver. For a start, he actually fought against the Nazis and secondly he didn't become a deep-sea diver in reality – he became an Officer in the R. A. F. So it just grew, evolved, this living spreadsheet, which was not an animal that reminds of wealth, but of grand-dad's generation and the horror of war.

My best guess is that it was to do with "Symbiotic Homeostasis." That means there was such a juxtaposition going on between Good and Evil that Nature acted with an homeostatic reaction. So we are talking about kinesis – but how crinoline became part of that kinesis I do not know. If you read my boyhood book, *The Sunset Child*, it contains the poem "Grand-darth's Ship" within a long sequence where there are at least four scientific functions, interwoven, while I am one of four children, who are born in a season each, going right left right left in the hands. The material was never tested but it could've been something my father passed on to me, the living spreadsheet; and he in turn might've got the word "crinoline" from grand-dad – but that I don't know.

It could be that my own knowledge of my own seven year old writing, my own memory of it, the human experience of writing it, was annexed into what became reified. That it was a literal invention that came from my mind but wasn't "an illusion" or "hallucination" – still I don't know this. I remember that the crinoline bit, that flat bed, was almost see-through and the size of a credit card except without rounded corners. The un-natural pattern of that rotten black stuff on top was what horrified me the most. It was regimented.

Here you might ship in knowledge of poetic form. How the theme "a clock is only as fast as a cheetah" even rhymes with "poetic metre." There seemed a great variety in my boyhood book, between poems that were neat and others done in a rush. Why it happened to me I don't know but it might've been my dad's business.

They say this is what I should've been writing about when I was writing teenage love poetry inspired by Jim Morrison – but it's better late than never eh?

They also say you shouldn't write about things you cannot renew; but I think in this case the synthesis of crinoline might be renewed even if not by me.

I also think if you can trust my sensory perception it shows that science is the key to a world of possibility. To possibilities opening up. It shows what can be done and that is surely inspiring. I am not trying to bring down the government or start a Revolution, only report accurately on what has been seen, sound out the realm of the senses. If new possibilities arise that is surely a good thing and should not be squashed or censored.

Actually, I take it back: I have no way of knowing the plastic spreadsheet was the substance crinoline. I just hoped that when I read my dad's notebook, there were answers. He left a list of French vocab that was a code encrypting the whole of the story. In a section entitled "Five Shapes" his vocab list included the English and French for crinoline. So it's not just that I have no way of knowing now but that he didn't either. So I have to shoulder the blame or even accept the praise for disposing of that revolting thing.

I'M FINE

"I'm fine," I say all the time and you wouldn't know what I mean.

I mean I was visibly marked on the hand by the experiment into the maths of the new colour as a cellular mark when I was about 11.

I took a long thin stripe up the underside, and that is what I mean when I say I'm fine.

It didn't turn out to be the new colour in the end.

We still see that it is possible to effect your own evolution.

You could even call it self-evolution.

This one might imagine comes from within as opposed to adaptation to the environment. It might be what Darwin would focus on in my situation, nevertheless: The Theory of Self-Evolution. And if I were a shapeshifter, Protean, a changeling, I would also try and be the Darwin of light, where maybe Morley is the Einstein of water.

JOHANNES BERGFORS

THE RED AND BLUE THING

Between the tincture and *The Road To Heaven by Noj And The Mob* there was a prose poem, or even dyad of prose poems called 'The Fire' and 'The Sea'. I was thus quite old when I "did the red and blue thing" and now through reading gather that it was yet another example of imbrocation with a scientist poet called David Morley, which I would see more of the older I got.

'The Fire' was a description of the sitting room fire, its 100 tongues that danced and entranced, here where the stars realign. It was observed; whereas 'The Sea' was remembered and imagined. It's interesting though because there is a difference between humidity and moisture in the air; and the hottest star heat burns blue; and the red and blue thing as they call it, which Michael Hofmann writes of in a poem called 'Entr' acte' could be but a graph with one long line kinking headward from the heart and ending in the stars.

So that was something I did between the tincture and the first album; and back then I was a garden brick expert – my garden bricks, attention to detail in grammar and spelling too, and general keen-ness at English saw me top of the form at English every term at school. And then years later, as I say, I found out at University that Professor David Morley had done the "red and blue thing" through the elements in just the same way, when he was studying acid rain's effect on Lake Windemere up in the Lakes where I lived as a child.

PHILOSOPHY FOR CHILDREN

Il faut que je m'en aille.

Sometimes you've just got to hit the road and.

Start learning the basics of a strange, unseen vernacular arrowed down from some lost, mad Godhead within. Pass the fallen road sign saying THINK! in the nettles and the mystery of the single shoe beside the road, in a fast Subaru Impreza with Paul and the gang, the Beatles' back catalogue tumbling from the speaker, the open window a roaring lion, late birds singing in trees, birds that are intelligent, trees that are our friends, on a smouldering evening in Cambridgeshire, when nothing really matters.

The Road To Heaven by Noj And The Mob. L to the pregnant snorkel + Ossie the dog, he should be sleeping like a log, goes round and round chasing his own tail, only goes upstairs for a trail of Maltesers, nice, round and pale, we're on the road to Heaven, happiness awaits us there, flutter in the sideways, flutter in the sideways, bring your brief fling with the politics of flight…

Teacher rite elephant nite

everything lite lesson love

learn tell everyone Esso orange.

2 MC = E = MC [someone] 1

In the picture of the airport

I can see... a runway,

a cloud, two planes,

a control tower

and the ire ii net.

In our new program there is a Vetacore.

A bomp explodes.

I faded my work.

I found a piece of string with a stone on it. I put it round my neck. I saw that the stone could fit into the hole in the wall. It was full of dead skeletons.

He has spines all over him.

Colour circles red. How many circles?

Colour triangles blue. How many squares?

Colour oblongs orange. How many triangles?

Hot July brings cooling showers,

straw berries and gilly flowers.

It was 6. 58 and 37 seconds so we all ran as fast as we could towards the sofa.

MY DOG HAS GOT NO BRAIN,

MY DOG IS A TOTAL PAIN,

HE'S GOT THREE EYES

AND A BIG FAT NOSE

AND GETS HIMSELF TANGLED

WITH THE GARDEN HOSE,

HE ONCE TOOK A PILL

THAT MADE HIM ILL

AND EVER SINCE THEN

HE'S BEEN STANDING VERY STILL.

Squawk squawk gaggle gaggle, bongles has still got the stones.

Sullen, silken sulks,

we drink the same rain,

spit is clean

and so is dirt.

Folder graffiti. Normal is boring. Do it later. God made speed to save us, God made hash to help us. The system works quite well. The grass is always long on the Other Side.

The fire-dance dwelled in electric drums

where ecstasy fell soft fathoms to clap

and bells let peace form in blue notes

and peered at deer in the wood and ate of it

and wet let excellence sound out its criticism

and dawn let sting its unsheathed sting

and chloroform in the heart let see

if only Game Over was seen in nights.

The

sun

hanged

himself

from

a

length

of

daisy

chain.

Clocktick clock being clocked off by clocktick.

Clocktick clock not being clocked off by Time.

The Universal Mind's moon meat man might.

The Universal Mind's moon meat man meant.

The Universal Mind's moon meat man met.

Break, bird with the skin of snake.

God rushed into the cold cod quick.

Behold! An evil vision hath flashed before mine eyes!

Barnes has scored a chicken

and wingers are allowed bikes!

Maybe a tabular arrangement of signs in boxes, like The Periodic Table except a swear word in every box, to go at the end.

Even A Duck Gets Big Erections: my mnemonic for the strings of the electric guitar took the same amount of time to conjure as it takes to say, but my mother has changed it now.

My name is David Bonky,

I'm a knock-kneed hummingbird,

there's a tear up my jacket.

Over and out, testing testing 123, welcome to my presence and its intensity...

I watch her walk along on the other side of the street.

She parades the black panther's nonchalant strut.

She wears blue jeans and black leather boots.

She takes some chewing gum out of her bag.

She slides the stick of it out of the pack.

She puts the stick of it into her mouth.

She loves to chew and suck the taste.

She loves to chew and suck the taste.

She puts the packet back in her bag.

She swings the bag about a little bit.

She walks past a little pub long shut.

She might go check out a flower shop.

She loves to chew and to suck the taste.

She enjoys it, chewing and sucking the taste.

I read that Maya means "Goddess of Illusion" in Sanskrit, where Mara, by stunning contrast, is the Buddhist God of Temptation.

A glance

A blink

A fault in the stars

Her mascara slips into pools of black

A chance

A second

    of Infinity

She flutters her eyelids

    like spring's first butterfly

The stars awake to notice love

she waits with open arms.

Sometimes I wish to have no more than a line penned in the margins of a newspaper going:

The light of all that's good is true

if believing is the dawn of dreams.

Only when the ship is ripped is the sea a she and the water Nirvana-blue as solar spike.

Desperate for sex with a dream full of ladies.

Desperate for sex with a dream full of ladies.

Soft

and

loose

like

yellow

pencils

scribbling

dreams

as

they

arrive.

Semen spills like silver water.

Don't escape at night

into a heightened dream

from a dull and longing sleep

gone where the stars murmur

their cool ballad

to the approaching sky

if it only means that

her breath a poisonous magic.

Sometimes perhaps

down opening quiet

I am drawn down

long and alone and

my friend and my foe

recede into deep sleep

sudden and still

like a dawn behind

a screaming veil

where silence is born

and all that's loose and tight

and all that's light is light

like first morning

with no night.

There is joy in things

and smiles not grins like butter

but like butterflies.

My philosophy in a nutshell: *sensus praecedit cogitationem*. It could be the motto of the LSE's Philosophy Dpt; but when you write it down, what happens?

Tonight it is your right to judge by heart alone.

When I first read the line "I look forward to the future with rapt uncertainty - and I can't stand the suspense," for some unknown reason it chimed like bells, reverberating up in the fells and struck a warm, psychic chord. I even conjured lines to rhyme with it before I knew what it meant like:

[John is dancing with aliens in collective ecstasy].

Blessed may be the end at last,

under the sea,

below the soul,

in the upside-down

Oceans above us

(all that Heaven sends is rain).

V to the knock-kneed hummingbird's wings… plus, in Rimbaud's colours of the vowels, E is white; but in my friend Agent G's musical code, when you detune the guitar strings all the way down, the streetname for E becomes F sharp minor!

2

JOHN TUCKER

ENGLISH

E

ENGLISH

JOHN TUCKER

HARECROFT

1

Signed by everwell, she couldn't hit it sideways, or maybe a soothsaying Spiderman with the hairgel of Dracula, Atlantis, Aquarius, the 60's.

Last night it seemed we couldn't

sleep but maybe I was dreaming.

The world expands inside my

hands it's getting heavy.

Of all the treasures I could

choose I can't seem to decide.

Today the shade was washed

away where I would hide.

Dream with open eyes, come

below and we can fantasise.

Now that I've stopped telling lies, come

below and we can fantasise.

Last night it seemed we nearly

died but maybe I was dreaming.

It made me feel sooooooooooooo

alive and soooooooo in love.

Dream with open eyes, come

below and we can fantasise.

Now that I've stopped telling lies, come

below and we can fantasise.

THE INVENTION OF HALFWARE

The idea of "steamed Apple juice" is in my dad's vision of the Future State and reminds me to write a note on invention. Sometimes inventions come good and sometimes not. If I could invent a pen-knife with any tools, Dr. Calculator Ptom's word chord synthesiser would be one, also a drug called Strictly Free that does exactly what it says on the tin, is and makes you strictly free to consume. A virtual death machine would be another, also a red-bleeding type-writer inside a ping-pong ball.

Maybe I'd trespass into the world of unseemly language and say an holographic horsepenis wheeled in to a corrupt politician's bedroom would also be possible. An invisible square of air called 'Mosaic by Darth Vader' stroked on telly could be another like an eco-poetic post-poem. I'd also like to invent a neutraliser drink that sobers you, totally, in an instant. At least I did when I dreamed up this pen-knife in the year 2000.

Further mad, Icelandic inventions would include the Nirvana button or pill, the Doors computer game, the psycho-sensitive fire alarm, a computer that speaks to you in the style of Rimbaud (translated by Mathieu), a gaseous camera and most recently an hyperlink to Heaven! What's wrong with these is that they are not real. It is better to relate than invent in art. Art is above politics. We should live in the here and now and real also as a Buddhist would say. My dad would tell me this, and tell me sci-fi is secondary to the human condition. He would tell me the more weird aliens you get in a film the worse it is.

There are inventions that are real, however. This brings me to the topic of halfware. Let me run you through a series of events. Firstly The Flood's binaural earphone album went online. Looking back, attempting to "plug my senses in the mains" via the album recorded on binaural earphones may have been folly, and I still find I can only receive and not send, here in this Age where we can send without form. When one of the numbers picked up a sensory overlay, a sophisticated arrhythmia, a clickety clickety clicking like something from Autechre, I started to entertain it was a quote, a sonic machination from *The Lords And The New Creatures*, the moment when "the chopper blazed over/ inward click and sure." My good friends in the band assured me it was nothing of the sort, more a technological quirk, and that may be where I went wrong, or they.

I still hear "the dark CD" we made in The Flood. I had a song called 'The Dark Carnival Dance' that we recorded but which didn't make it to the 6-song album or even playlist. But the sense of dark is as in dark matter when you record on binaural earphones. Because of the way it all worked, the promise to plug my senses in the mains, I hear music in the dishwasher going round. Sound travels and travels far and wide. My Floyd was very Freud.

As for healing the tape with the pause where cut and stuck together in the reel in a delicate operation, the tape didn't start as mine, so I don't qualify it as my own "property." I can say its successful fusion may have combined two things:

1. my grand-dad's motto "the mustard has to be English."

2. my knowing the Thai for the tacky, 1990's pop song 'There's No Limit.'

When after years the fusion was (somehow) successful it became an objet d'art, a Strange Attractor, a dream-meet connector, an Utilitarian Martianist wedding ring that lived beneath my pillow and propitiated dreams of things like "The Ninero Ratio." Still, one night as the wind enwheeled through the dark garden trees and an alchemical, base metal feeling pervaded my soul I remembered the formula for mud from Primary School:

water + soil = mud

and by now having gone mad went downstairs and cooked the cassette tape, the evidence in the dark blue AGA, top oven, hottest one. I still think as my dad said it was then that it became "a valid work of art," which I dutifully photo'd and put online somewhere

As for the numinous purple bleeding screen, its colour was co-aligned with mystery, sex, *suadade*, longing and shame thus to incorporate every vowel-sound into a feeling.

All these examples and more I would contend could be considered "halfware." There was at the time also an exploded telegraph pole and more and many more and they said my name was tattooed on *Piper* and I was still trying to write songs.

So we see that there is a distinction in invention between that which is actualised and that which remains a pipe dream. If the early pen-knife tools I mention remained pipe dreams there were things of note in the realm of invention that were actualised and which I consider "halfware."

It could even be instructive to consider that living spreadsheet I mention as Halfware too. All this just goes to show that today's science-fiction is tomorrow's real science. The quark is laughing in eternity.

TRANSITION TO PHILOSOPHY VOLUME THREE

TREATMENT OF P

I feel that in the previous two volumes I attained the transition to philosophy successfully and herein have taken on an ambitious task in my treatment of P. Something about the running order of the phrase lends itself to peace. The repetition of the mouth-sounds "he found" at the start of every line in that piece, that fragment lends itself to the phrase "he found peace." If I might reiterate the point one more time...

He found himself on a plane.

He found himself on a.

He found himself on.

He found himself.

He found.

P.

Privacy wouldn't do it, nor personality, as in the personality of the author. Nor "this is a present." Nor, say, prison, perfection, prattling voices, parsimony, pentimento, plasticity of rock, or prudence. My final answer is peace and if it is also "proposition" it would still be peace, it would be "May peace and peace and peace be everywhere."

Hardly a proposition as we know it, however, the P itself detonates millions of ramifications across the board. Ultimately peace is the most important one of those ramifications. Poetry is another sense; and I have also looked into the dawn chorus of the pterodactyls – into pterodactyl wings – but nothing will satisfy the reader as much as inner peace. We must, as Neil Curry suggests, make peace with the certitude of loss, as much as with our selves; and what with the political climate in the world right now threatening to spill over, peace is the lesson from John – who uses the philosophy pen-name Johannes – this morning. If you want to say P is for Paul I can method act that poem, for I did, upon leaving Dr. Calculator Ptom's school, find Paul so to speak – but I cannot endorse or recommend peace highly enough, so that is my final answer. Peace.

So I watch the wind blowing the long grass that duly sways with it out in the Gondwanaland-green garden out the back at dawn on a summer morning, and commend Dr. Calculator Ptom if that is who it is as I think, as I believe, for holding the infinite in but a letter! Never before have I seen such terse containment and it indicates a level of mathematical ability that is beyond mine own. The piece proceeds like an algorithm, or process of elimination, narrowing down to a singular point of understated beauty, humility, humanity, and containing as much ambiguity as can be done. So many different senses of P all in one example. So many heterogeneous examples summarised in one fell swoop. The waves are averaged out. The subject in question is where something becomes one and countable. I thank Dr. Ptom for his message, sent through the vibrant, new air.

He found himself on a plane.

He found himself on a.

He found himself on.

He found himself.

He found.

P.

And was it functionality that drew me to this? I would reiterate Wilde and say of use and beauty if it has no use it must be art. Dr. Ptom reached into his plectrum pocket when he was on the plane and brought out a plectrum. With it he had strummed a guitar many times. He wouldn't mind being in his own work if it turned out that he was a Guinness – and it has and he is. What has been said within these pages is enough to qualify his genius. Then all of a sudden P is for "paradigm shift" and reminds us of September 11th; then all of a sudden it is for *Paradise Lost*! When I hooked up with Dr. Ptom a few years back in London at another school reunion, he said "I don't see how you can write poetry unless you've read *Paradise Lost*." He was reading things like *Lolita* at 13!

I soon read Milton's sublime epic poem! I still in all "probability" haven't caught Dr. Ptom up with my reading list despite reaching a saturation point. Perhaps the point is that the wing-bit is the proposition in a postmodern way? Perhaps it is postmodern text-art? There is a school of poets, poets, b/t/w/, interested in sending text messages into space. I was one of them. I used to text free association, spontaneous writing like Jack Kerouack in digital miniaturism into space... but this text-art is a different sense of text, as in lexicographic, and also a different sense of "send" as in "project" – without form – without hands other than the other person, person on the other end. He used my hands to send me a text. From miles away. So you could say the school is an Informationist school; but the words themselves – they are smooth as marble cherubim.

Just for a second P is for press. It is not to press self-destruct though, nor is it to press a button that does away with mental health issues. It is to press "send" which amounts to "receive." I find that a post-Eliotious tone of mind. But TS Eliot contains no 'P.' For the right P in the literary world we might need to see Thomas Pynchon who wrote *Gravity's Rainbow* that so influenced our Dr. Ptom.

He found himself on a plane.

He found himself on a.

He found himself on.

He found himself.

He found.

P.

Dr. Ptom says philosophy is a sterile subject. He got that from the time he said to me "the universe is a projection of the mind," and I said back: "I've thought of a more poetic way of saying it. The sniper's rifle is an extension of his eye." The incident is already in a previous volume. And what about Publicity? He found publicity? Or publication? There is something strong about Dr. Ptom's "proposition" that could drive a line all the way to publication in a self-perpetuating motion. And what about *Paradise Regained*? I haven't read that one yet. Projection. It must be projection. Not to dampen the plea for world peace but it must be projection, because of the way it was sent: form and content become one. "The medium is the message" as MacLuhan said. Touch is the shortest route between subject and object. He touched my qwerty keypad with my fingers. Then the infinite was held in the colloquial. Then the abstract and concrete were united. Then we all lived happily ever after. Ounce upon a tome, I should re-begin, but won't.

I'll just say: Philosophy – it might have died. Philosophy – crossed to the other side. But when there are friendships as strong as Dr. Ptom and I, and minds keen enough to question things, the way we use language for example, the way we write, then philosophy lives on and that is to be taken as a triumph of the human spirit, and not to be taken as a sentence to spend in a library corner researching the meanings of words. So it is that through liberating another's genius we find our own, through kindness, and all exemplums of pretty rhetoric flail against the rocks like sloppy waves compared with the genome intact of the parcel I was sent by an old friend who devastates the connection between the stars to unite. Through whom but the room do the people come and go Smart-talking of Hume on the grand piano? O Ptom, come down from the mountainsides glad, come down from the clouds, the school bus, the treetop, the FTSE 100, the Towers, the musical instrument between the stars has grown random with random access co-imagination and the help that is at hand has been a hand in a band and to scar sand-birthmarks beneath my skin was once deemed vogue and to be within.

I tried it and liked it, thinking of you, and maths without answers, me over you, Times by Telegraph, love over gold, self-undermining and much that is untold. Now in the morning, turning to face you, I wish for a connection, that has no words, not telepathy, not ESP, a no word connection, free. Any more of that sweet poesis flow, it would defeat the point of the new pen-name, of the ironic self-distance, of getting away from the bad habit and habitat, the adolescent landscape. This morning I am happier than I have been for a long time, and await the publication of the first two volumes, sipping on tepid tea and insufflating the fume of the Vape pen. Pens! Maybe within the relay, the system, my every use of words beginning with P is a guess in the right direction, but made purposefully by the unconscious. Someone mentions my getting a blue plaque for this, and I think of Orwell. I am not him and he is not me. I am Johannes Bergfors, aka John F B Tucker, on 17/ 06/ 2025, Cumbria.

He found himself on a plane.

He found himself on a.

He found himself on.

He found himself.

He found.

P.

JOHANNES BERGFORS

FURTHER TREATMENT OF P

You notice here that the plane from the first line is attained at the end, like a plane of consciousness, in P. In philosophy they ask whether a proposition "obtains" and I think this one does but in a way crosses a boundary between sense and the preverbal; between meaning and the primitive; and I would say it journeys from Signification to Significance. It could also be said to make significance from insignificance. But this idea of crossing a border is what I like. As the line lengths narrow down, as silence triumphs bit by bit, we have both meaning and the pictorial combined. The sense of the first sentence displays both. Without the sense that is in the first sentence there is no "picture" nor therefore any "meaning". The poem would not obtain, nor denote anything like a plane wing. The last line, the singular P, is not only a removal of sense in the traditional sense of the mechanics of meaning, but a summary of the picture as a whole. So when I say it removes sense (as it removes the third person protagonist), it also confirms sense in a more suggestive way.

To settle on peace as before, one starts to consider that there is more. In one sense everything the third person protagonist has is being systematically taken away from him, until he attains some kind of numbness or maybe even triumph at the end. In another sense there are moments in making that journey such as the sentence "he found himself" that strike one not so much as the protagonist being deprived of securities as him winning the battle. It is a most fascinating piece of literature, even if it doesn't work out loud, and awakens one to the potential of the new word in the new world.

When I say it doesn't work out loud, that's because you don't get the physical shape of it through

Oral means; so this leads me to consider that the wing-bit might not be poetry at all. But that is a very reductive and old-fashioned attitude perhaps? There are of course bits that only work orally: "he found himself on a:" that second line: the word "honour" carries to the mind's ear through enjambment and adds another touch to this exciting circuit. One would suppose that there is an extent to which meaning in the poem is down to Chance. But when you get to the end is it down to Fate? And when I call it a poem, it might not be that, but a philosophical proposition as earlier mentioned. Does the P stand for the 1p that the witness never attained for his work?

He found himself on a plane.

He found himself on a.

He found himself on.

He found himself.

He found.

P.

Or is it the fact that the plane crashed into the nerve-centre of money? There seems a closure of a gap going on, a removal of distance; and also of note there is stunning contrast between the meaningful sense of plane as in he found himself on a plane (of consciousness) and the meaningful sense of the shape as a literal plane.

One further point could be that as the poet Simon Pomery contends, poets have the ability to put their finger on another's heart-valve. The ambiguity as to the sense of plane runs through Dr. Ptom's wing-bit; and my knowing it was him shows how close we were, shows this very act of putting a finger on another's heart-valve. Portability as an aesthetic is contained; pulse is also contained. As the border is crossed from the pictorial to the sensical, the senses of the word "plane" also swap around. Does life empty itself of meaning the older you get? Or does the universe just become an ever-more mysterious place?

Answers on the back of a postage stamp may not get us very far but Dr. Ptom's wing-bit is terse and one might even argue "Smart." It could be a Smart-poem if you [permit] such a thing. For the word digital also corresponds to the fingers and once again, he touched my qwerty keypad with my fingers.

Any treatment of P cannot forget that what goes up must come down. Also, America is mobilising its Air Force while I write, unbeknownst to me for the most of it. If only there were a way to guarantee peace with a piece of writing. It's really distressing waiting for Donald Trump to make a decision as to whether or not to attack Iran. I had a dream, where Kurt Cobain gave me some heroin. I woke in the night-time, remembering days and games and daisy chains and laughs – Cambridge. I was thinking of musical concepts again – back in the self-conception of being a young musician. But an awful feeling suddenly overcame me once more and tuning in I remembered it was war. I had to check BBC News online for updates. Nobody knows what to do with the News.

There were loads of things going on in my musical life once upon a time – recording on earphones, healing the tape of its pause where resealed in the reel, the effervescent mobile, writing a paper on whether Lucy in the soul w/ demons is an actual substance, and eventually I would discover the sheet where pictures grew – not to mention all the songs I have written. Re-waking palely tonight a narrowing down, a compression forced me into a blue mood. To pick up the guitar is useless. To advertise my musical concepts herein is useless. I don't feel very well, and yet feel pity for a mental health professional who has to listen to and deal with others' woes in times like these. Meanwhile youth has drained from me and its energy too.

So it is that the symbol, figment or image of the wing-bit goes from allusion to yesterday's terrorist attacks to tomorrow's potential invasion of Iran. Friends are good and I miss mine. I think of a present tense friend wallowing in depression, how I feel sorry for him and am here for him, how often he goes on holiday, the paintings of his I have in my room, the music we recorded but never yet organised into an album, the way sometimes our conversations about art feel like a license to print money.

He found himself on a plane.

He found himself on a.

He found himself on.

He found himself.

He found.

P.

In short, someone left the window open and now the house is overrun with flies. In short, the image is the most international currency. In short in times like these you wonder what is the international language for words such as "this decision to make war is a violation of the sanctity of the human spirit. It is a deradicalisation of a unilateral contract that means being human." I have entertained that P is for "person." We cannot forget that in these troubled and testing times.

SOUP

I remember when we were playing touch rugby – the lads in the team – in training – and I sold someone a dummy and made a bid for freedom, escapism down the right wing... after the training session there was a packet of thigh bones and some breast in the supermarket and I'm telling you man, the thigh bones were more expensive per pound than the breast. By now I might need specs and to see the new creatures has been deemed such a sin that I continued my escape down the right. I wasn't bad at rugby. Dr. Ptom was a hooker, I was a back. I found a wishing bone. We'll see what happens. If she doesn't pay me she can kiss her holiday goodbye. One of our clients keeps inviting me. She has a financial advisor who pulled the whole of the Nat West bank up from bankruptcy. I've been speaking to him about tax – and am on the borderline. Now I'm making soup, it's just what I am doing. I love you. It might be more a stew than a soup. There's a naturally purple sweet potato that goes in it – is that what Hendrix would be eating? This one smells of chrysanthemums. My back is hurting. It's fairly salty. I am going to need some milk or cream or something in it.

JOHANNES BERGFORS

THE OTHER SIDE

When I came out the other side I was desperate for coffee. We went to a cafe, Dr. Ptom and I and discussed what we had learned. He didn't like the way the protagonist had dyed it. Nor the Revolutionary imagery he had been privy to either. We conversed for a long time in the cafe over coffee and Danish pastries. Then I told him I loved him and we parted, went our separate ways. Then in time to come one would imagine that

He found himself on a plane.

He found himself on a.

He found himself on.

He found himself.

He found.

P.

P by now was for pot so he went into the plane toilet and smoked a bifter on the plane. There was a smoke detector which he thought was an extractor fan so he blew great plumes of smoke directly into it. In fact he was going to Amsterdam: a place where traditionally persecuted or censored philosophers go to find freedom of expression. He got off the plane, took a neat train into the CNS of the city, and as he disembarked said to himself: "I am a philosopher. I am, I can."

He thought to himself that he should eat something and headed for a food place. There was a band playing live... ladies and gentlemen, Lords and New Creatures, please welcome to the stage a great act... I give you Oedipus Wrecks.

THE OEDIPUS WRECKS GIG, CAMDEN TOWN, CIRCA 1998

I

SECRETS IN THE MUD

This is the sound of getting totally fucked.

Of when you first get your notebook sucked.

Of changing gold into Glastonbury mud.

Of lying down in a field with your bud.

This is the music through whom we aspire.

This is the rule book that is thrown on the fire.

This is the jam where the trousers are down.

This is the wine-shop on the edge of town.

Chorus: Glastonbury, you should be free, and all you have in your big city,

you hit my G, you make me see how I want to see,

lights go down, lights come on,

and all my sadness seems to be gone,

although I still love to be what I dream I am.

[guitar solo]

II

OCEANS SMILE

Oceans smile with liquid eyes

and fill themselves with rain.

The tide goes out and leaves me

lost, the last thing a glass gene.

Follow me to the resurrection

while the blind get crucified.

My weapon's only loaded in my eyes.

Death will come on silky wings

but I for one will not go.

A soul is endless, oceans open

and keeeeeeeps a perfect O.

Follow me to the resurrection

while the blind get crucified.

My weapon's only loaded in my eyes.

Go drink the ocean with your tea

cup, give your heart far out.

If oceans smile with liquid eyes

then they'll give you a shout.

Follow me to the resurrection

while the blind get crucified.

My weapon's only loaded in my eyes.

Too drunkenly I sail the water

on Rimbaud's smoking boat.

With whiskygills primed in fire

I sail the waves to Boot.

Follow me to the resurrection

while the blind get crucified.

My weapon's only loaded in my eyes.

(reconstructed via the new, synchronised word)

III

KILL

My eyes sting,

my teeth are bleeding raw,

too much thought

to make me sick.

Stinky clothes

and mouth become

my skin and all

these fruits I want to kill.

Give my hope,

surrender to the tide,

you can take

my remains;

but I must go,

to wash the poison

from my eyes,

before, before, before I kill.

IV

SNAKE SNAKE BUTTERFLY

Snake snake butterfly, lay me dead & close my eyes.

Angel serpentine, she waits on the Other Side.

Give me your alibi; give me chains to stop me fly;

give me night to soothe my blinded eyes:

so I can see the secrets of the skies.

We must rise, freedom falling from our eyes,

unlock doors, it's a perfect time to die,

and it's okay 'cause baby we'll go insane

but don't reach out too far for the flame.

Snake snake butterfly, lead me to the Other Side.

Angel serpentine, she waits on the Other Side.

V

VITAL SIGNS

Smile like a smile just to smile,

cast to Heaven for a while...

let's rip holes in the boat,

throw the captain overboard,

throw the angels off the bridge,

death comes and stops me getting

bored of life's soul-machine.

What we need is energy,

show me all your vital signs,

what we steal is what we need,

what we need to feel alive,

for I'm alive with vital signs.

Back to Hell to plunder wings,

let the ritual now begin,

come and ride the waiting beast,

ride it gone into the fire,

ride it to the waiting feast,

my baby's waiting to get higher,

to get higher, to get higher...

what we need is energy,

show me all your vital signs,

what we steal is what we need,

what we need to feel alive,

for I'm alive with vital signs,

yeah feel alive with vital signs.

Come again there's much to do,

don't you know that I love you?

VI

HEAVEN KNOWS

Heaven knows and walks away -

but what it knows it will not say.

It's impossible to make a cowboy film in space?

Heaven knows and turns its face!

Heaven's filled with silver eyes.

Heaven's hills all harmonise.

I hear its angels when they call...

Heaven knows and lets them fall!

[reconstructed]

VII

MURDER IS DEAD

Fuck this, fuck that, fuck me yeah,

I wish that I had been there,

been there to saaaaaave Jesus,

I'm sure he meant to please us.

Murder is dead,

murder is dead,

murder is dead.

We're young and filled with semen,

we're going to break some hymen,

we'll make the cops turn in their badges,

we're going over all the edges yeah.

Murder is dead,

murder is dead,

murder is dead.

VIII

THE GHOSTS LAMENT (THE GUZZLER MEN)

I'm the only one left, left to shoot my

own gun. This is the dead land. Crack a smile

and curse the sun. Death awaits to fuck me.

Give me bliss and give me kisses. Death a-

waits to save me. The ghosts lament, the ghosts

lament. Come on baaaaaaaaaby, you know it's e-

asy, don't say maaaaaaaaaybe, let's go crazy. Death

awaits to fuck me. Give me bliss and give

me kisses. Death awaits the same me. The

ghosts lament, the ghosts lament, no more ghosts.

||||.

I KNEW THAT SHE LOVED ME

I escaped last night

into a heightened dream

from a dull and longing sleep

and the stars murmured

their cool ballad

to the approaching sky.

Secrets hung like ghosts

in the corner of my wanton world

all blurred and drugged too deep

and I knew that she loved me

from her invisible motions

and the dagger in her soft reply.

The questions concealed in her eye.

Her smile a luring prison.

Her blink a beautiful danger.

Her breath a poisonous magic.

And I knew that silence

would soon let slip its whisper,

knew that fantasy

had never been so real

and I knew that she loved me

because I knew everything.

I knew.

ACROSS THE SEA OF TEA

Even to defend the Feds would normally be against my principles like monopolising indigenous wisdom in regimented metres; but if the Feds defended me, saved me, when I was in a rather difficult situation, it would therefore not be true that the Feds are evil.

If you're about to die and the Feds save your life it is specious that they are evil.

They might hold a monopoly on evolution; which is why Jim Morrison's book *The Lords And The New Creatures* – taken as a bet, or a test – is an interesting media-compression experiment; but that doesn't mean they are evil.

They may have good reasons for trying to maintain Order and Balance, and know things we can not know.

If the Feds ask you to incorporate a piece, say, a rehashing of The Road To Heaven by Noj And The Mob, you should do it, even if the piece is not very good, because it might just be a token of your gratitude, or a signifier of good intention.

It might be for instance the principle of your obeying them that they want to be observed in which case it would not be evil of you to humour their intentions.

If at the same time your brother doesn't wish for his notion concerning <BEE> coming after @ in the international language alphabet to incur the problem of regression by the revisit to your childhood, it would be manners to leave that out for now.

EPILOGUE

And what about Hannah Dear? She says (as my first volume reported) that I wasn't the only one privy to Morrison's reveal; but I was the only one who also helped invent the net at seven with government scientists – and I can't do BOTH. Well, what is in the past I cannot control but I can say I haven't met any new creatures for many years, nor do I appear ostensibly to be a government scientist. So I can report on what has gone on as background, without necessarily making a double claim that is perceived as being hypocritical. So it is that I bring this volume to a close and point your extended gaze further on to the possibility of future work from me… there is already a fourth volume underway but I will keep its contents secret as whispers and kisses for now.

ABOUT THE AUTHOR

Johannes Bergfors (which is the philosophy name of John F B Tucker) was born in London in 1982 to a Finnish mother and an English father. He got a First Class Honours degree in English, Creative Writing and Practise from Lancaster University in 2009. He now lives in Cumbria, at the foot of Black Combe, with his mother and brother.

www.ingramcontent.com/pod-product-compliance
Lightning Source LLC
Chambersburg PA
CBHW031145160426
43193CB00008B/263